His~~~~~~~~~~~~
Ancient Rome

www.dinobibi.com

Contents

Introduction

Rome will always be important in history and culture. For over 2000 years, Rome has continued to influence, or impact, our world with its rich past and colorful history. The discussion about Ancient Rome and its influence on Modern Rome and the larger modern world will never get old.

Rome has affected the modern world in many ways. Ancient Rome was a powerful and important civilization that ruled almost all Europe for nearly a thousand years. Ancient Rome's culture spread throughout Europe during the period it ruled. As a result, Ancient Rome and its culture are important in the Western world today. Many aspects of Western culture come from Ancient Rome, especially in areas such as government, engineering, architecture, language, and literature.

To ignore Rome would be to ignore much of the history that laid the groundwork for our world. At its peak, Ancient Rome ruled over most of continental Europe, Britain, much of western Asia, northern Africa, and the lands of the Mediterranean.

Roman Empire XXL

The effect of the Roman Empire's dominance across history is evident in how it forms the bedrock of many of the biggest languages in the world today, including Italian, Spanish, French, and Portuguese, as well as other languages derived from Latin. The Ides of March, for example, is marked as a day in the **Roman calendar** (15th March). Historically, it is notable as the deadline the Romans set for settling debts and is marked by several **religious observances**. This date is the day that Julius Caesar was killed. For this reason, the Ides of March became a major decisive moment in history.

London, a historic city itself and the capital of today's England (and by extension United Kingdom) is also tied to Ancient Rome. In fact, its status as one of the most iconic places in the world is because the Ancient Romans made it the capital of Britannia when it was still a province of Rome. Also, the modern Western alphabet, the calendar we use today, and the emergence of Christianity as a major world religion have strong ties to Ancient Rome which further underlines how important Ancient Roman history is to today's world.

This book is a children-friendly account of how Ancient Rome began, grew to enormous heights, sustained its status, and then fell. While it can be challenging to take on this topic of Ancient Rome, seeing as there is no single story of the iconic city, and also the fact that the Roman Empire expanded much beyond Italy by a great deal, this book presents the topic in fun, engaging, and easy-to-read prose.

Chapter 1:
Origin Stories of Rome

There are several accounts of the origin and beginning of Ancient Rome. Two stories are most popular: The Founding Myth account which says that the two demi-god brothers, Romulus and Remus, founded Rome. There is also the story of Roma who escaped Troy with some survivors after its fall and had Rome named after her. Let's recap the two accounts in detail.

The Founding Myth

According to this account, Rome was founded on the banks of River Tiber in the middle of Italy. Romulus and Remus were the sons of Mars, the Roman god of war. Their mother, Rhea Silva was a mortal and their father was Mars, and so they were demigods (half-man, half-god). Rhea Silva was the daughter of Numitor, the Latin king of Alba Longa, an ancient Latin city in the Middle of Italy. During Rhea Silva's pregnancy and birth of the twins, the king's own brother, Amulius, overthrew King Numitor. Amulius, the new King, was afraid that the two princes, Romulus and Remus, would later grow up to avenge their father and win back the throne, so he ordered for them to be drowned in the River Tiber.

Romulus and Remus

The vessel they were placed in later drifted all the way ashore on the other end of the river, on a site that later became Rome. Some accounts say that a she-wolf nursed the baby boys and then a shepherd later raised them. In other accounts, a shepherd's wife rescued the boys from the river. When Remus and Romulus grew up, sure enough, they eventually headed back to Alba Longa to win back the throne. The brothers succeeded and returned rulership to King Numitor. The brothers left to found their own city, but they ended up quarreling about where their city would be located.

9

Some people believe the quarrel was about who was going to name and rule the city. Romulus killed his brother Remus and went on to locate the city on the Palatine Hill. He also named the city after himself and crowned himself its first king.

For all its glory today, Rome first started out as a city for the downtrodden. King Romulus opened his city to people exiled from other cities. Rome was initially a city for unwanted and runaway people. Due to this, it quickly became a big city. While this would be a good thing under normal circumstances, it caused a problem because its inhabitants were mostly men and there were no women in the city. King Romulus tried to solve this problem by going into neighboring towns and cities to get women to marry his city's men, but failed. Rome was a city of the unwanted, so nobody wanted to be associated in such a permanent union with such people. Some people believe that the King Romulus later lured the people of Sabine to a festival, stole their unmarried women, and married them to his people.

The Myth of Roma

In this account, after the fall of Troy during the Trojan War, some Trojan survivors left intending to rebuild

Troy in a new location which they would call the new Troy. They sailed and sailed for a long time with no land in sight. The seas were very tumultuous and their journey was rough. It was a very long time before they arrived at the banks of the River Tiber. When they arrived, they camped there for a while and then the men wanted to head back out to sea. The problem was that women who were with them were weary and did not want to continue the journey, so they protested. During the conflict, a woman named Roma convinced the other women to burn every ship they had travelled with so there would be no way to leave again—or at least any time soon. After the women succeeded, the men were furious with Roma and wanted to punish her, but soon they realized that they did not have to leave. Their location was favorable and comfortable enough for them, and so they decided to stay. In gratitude to Roma who had forced them to realize this, they named the city that they formed after her.

There is also yet another notable origin account: The "Aeneid" classical poem. This account ties the founding myth and the myth of Roma together. In a poem titled "Aeneid" by Virgil, a poet, there is a prophesy that the Trojan Prince Aeneas is destined to found a new Troy. Prince Aeneas wanted to marry a beautiful woman called Lavinia. Lavinia was engaged to Turnus, the King of the Rutuli people. Prince Aeneas disagreed, so he challenged Turnus to war and won. He then travelled to Italy, where he became the ancestor of the Romans. According to this account, the Alban Kings (that is, the Kings of Alba Longa, which Romulus and Remus' mother descended from), are descendants of Prince Aeneas. Going by the account, Rome descended from Troy.

Opening lines of poem "Aeneid" written in Latin by Virgil

Early Ancient Rome

Not long after Rome was founded, the city started to grow. Trading was its chief source of income. Rome's location was easily accessible by both sailors and merchants, which made it easier for its economy to expand. During this period of growth, there were seven kings of Rome; these kings were Romulus, Numa Pompilius, Tullus Hostilius, Ancus Marcius, Lucius Tarquinius Priscus, Servius Tullius, and Lucius Tarquinius Superbus. The Romans borrowed some aspects of Greek culture like religion, literacy, and fundamental architecture. They also borrowed some principles of trade and urban luxury from the Etruscans. The Romans had a gift for borrowing ideas and improving them, so they grew faster than other cities around them. Between the 800BC and 600BC, they established themselves as a prosperous city.

Overthrow of the Roman Monarchy

A **monarchy** is a government where a single person has supreme authority. This person is known as a monarch. Monarchs use such titles as king, queen, emperor, or empress. Monarchies were once common throughout the world, but now they are rare. Monarchs typically reign for life. Also, they inherit the throne.

Tarquinius Superbus making himself King

The first seven kings of Rome were monarchs. In 509 BCE, during the reign of the last monarch, Lucius Tarquinius Superbus, his nephew Lucius Junius Brutus inspired a revolt and overthrew the Roman monarchy. Brutus had always hated King Tarquinius Superbus. Nicknamed Tarquinius the Proud, Lucius Tarquinius Superbus was a very wicked tyrant. He had ordered several Roman chiefs killed, one of whom was Brutus' brother.

Lucius Junius Brutus

Brutus led a rebellion against King Tarquinius Superbus after a noblewoman had been attacked by the king's son. The noblewoman, whose name was Lucretia, believed that the incident dishonored her so she stabbed herself to death. Brutus picked up the dagger and called for the King to be dethroned.

The people agreed with Brutus and voted that King Tarquinius Superbus and his family should be removed from power and banished. The Romans refused King Superbus and his family after being expelled from the army, so they went into exile.

After this, Brutus made the Romans to swear that no one would ever allow any man again to be king. He brought a new kind of government called a **republic**. In the new Roman republic, only representatives of the people had the right to pass laws and elect judges. These elected judges would have limited power and would only serve for a year each. These judges were called magistrates. The two most senior magistrates were called the consuls. The first two consuls were Brutus and the late Lucretia's husband, Lucius Tarquinius Collatinus.

Rome first grew into power as a republic. Rome's leaders were elected officials who served for a limited amount of time rather than inherited rulers who were born into leadership and had authority for life.

In the year 450 BC, the Romans agreed on a law called the First Roman Law Code. They wrote these laws on 12 tablets made of bronze and displayed it in a public place at the center of their city. They displayed these laws in a place called the **Roman Forum.** Their constitution made sure there was a balance of powers. These concepts have influenced other cultures throughout history. The Roman system of constitution is what formed the foundation for future democratic governments, such as the kind of government that the United States currently operates.

Roman Forum as it stands today

Chapter 2:
The Roman Republic

After King Tarquinius Superbus was overthrown, Lucius Junius Brutus and Collatinus were able to convince the Roman senate and the army to abolish kingship and swear never to allow any other king rule them. Many of the king's former functions transferred to Brutus and Collatinus who served as the first two consuls of the Roman Republic. The idea for having the two-man consulship was so no single man would have complete power. If a consul abused his powers in office, he could be prosecuted when his term expired. Shortly after, the Romans couldn't trust Collatinus because, even though he played an important role in the overthrow of the monarchy, he was a part of the family. The Romans forced him to resign from his consulship and leave Rome. They elected another consul to replace him. The third Roman consul history was a man named Publius Valerius Publicola.

The Romans enjoyed Republic life for a while, but after some time the old tyrant, Tarquinius Superbus, tried to reclaim the throne. He made three attempts. The first time he tried to win back the throne, he did it through a conspiracy, the second and third times, he tried to win back the throne by waging war on Rome. All three attempts failed.

The Tarquinian Conspiracy

The Tarquinian Conspiracy refers to the first time Tarquinius Superbus tried to take back the Roman throne. He sent ambassadors to Rome to request the return of his family property which they had left behind while fleeing to exile. Of course, the king wasn't really interested in getting his personal belongings back. Instead, he used these negotiations as a cover-up for his real plan. So, while the Roman senators considered the request of the ambassadors, the ambassadors convinced several Roman government officials to support the exiled king. They were even able to convert Lucius Junius Brutus' two sons, Titus and Tiberius, and also his brothers-in-law. While this was going on, the Roman senate accepted the ambassadors' requests to return the exiled king's personal belongings, but they soon realized that is was all a cover-up. Soon, the conspiracy was exposed. The Romans turned down the request and instead handed over the Royal personal belongings to the public to do with as they liked.

A slave who witnessed one of the meetings of the ambassadors with the Roman traitors exposed the conspiracy. Once he uncovered the conspiracy, the ambassadors were arrested but later released due to the laws across nations. However, the Roman conspirators who had started supporting the exiled King Tarquinius Superbus were condemned to death, including Brutus' sons. The traitors were undressed and flogged, then later they were beheaded (their heads were cut off in public). Brutus watched as his sons' heads were cut off; he didn't object to their execution. Some historians believe he cried out as their heads were cut off while others believed that he watched silently.

Execution of the sons of Lucius Junius Brutus, published 1878

The slave who exposed the conspiracy received freedom, citizenship, and with money for his role in spoiling the plans that would have made the tyrant come back into power.

The Battle of Silva Arsia and the Death of Brutus

This battle was the second attempt by the exiled king Tarquinius Superbus to regain power in 509 BC. The exiled king had won allies to his cause and attacked the Romans. The battle took place in a place called Silver Arsia (the Arsian forest). During the battle, Arruns, one of the sons of Tarquinius Superbus charged at Brutus. They fought with spears and killed each other. In the end, the Romans won the battle and chased the exiled king's army away.

After celebrating the victory, they brought back Lucius Junius Brutus' body to Rome and conducted a magnificent burial for him.

War with Clusium

This war was the third attempt of the exiled King Tarquinius Superbus to win back the throne. In 508 BC, one year after he lost the battle of Silva Arsia, he convinced King Lars Porsena, the king of Clusium, to go to battle with him against the Romans. Clusium had a fearsome army which made the Roman afraid. Fearing that the Romans would surrender to the Clusium-Superbus army, the senate made grains and salt cheaper and removed taxes from people of the lower classes. These actions made the people more loyal to the Roman senate, so they turned against the Clusium-Superbus army.

As the Clusium army attacked Rome, a soldier named Publius Horatius Cocles jumped across the bridge and fought bravely to buy the Romans time to burn the bridge. Two other brave soldiers, Titus Aquillius and Spurius Lartius, joined him. They were successful in defending the city. There were several other attacks, but eventually the war ended. The war probably ended with a peace treaty.

Government of the Roman Republic

For Rome to become a great city, the Romans needed a stable government. When the monarchy fell, the Romans had to swear they would never allow a single man to rule them again. So, they needed to find a way to separate authority in a way that was agreeable with everyone. Also, they needed to prevent anyone from ever seizing power again. The solution was to create a Republic.

Unfortunately, the journey to creating a true balance of power was not a smooth one. At first, in trying to separate powers, only the wealthy families, **patricians**, were in control of the republic. The word 'patrician' comes from the Latin word patres. At some point, only rich families could hold political appointments. The lower class of the Romans, **plebeians,** could not do anything about it. Some of the plebeians who became rich could not hold any political authority even if they were as wealthy as the patricians.

After some time, the plebians could not take it anymore. They felt it was unfair that no matter what they did or what they achieved, they could never have authority. They were annoyed that even though they provided the larger part of the army, they were treated like second-class citizens. They asked themselves why they would go to war when it was the patricians that would gain the glory. So, because of these complaints, they started causing trouble.

Finally, in the year 494 BC, the plebians went on strike. They gathered in the mountains outside Rome and refused to leave unless they were also allowed to rule. They demanded to be represented in running the affairs of the city. This strike is known as the **Conflict of Orders**. Another name for the Conflict of Orders was the **First Succession of the Plebs.** The strike lasted for a while until the patricians finally gave in. The plebians were finally rewarded with an assembly to represent them. This assembly became known as **Concilium Plebis**. Concilium Plebis means **Council of the Plebs.**

19th Century engraving about Revolt of Plebeians

Through the rebellion, the plebians were able to create a system where power lay in their magistrates and assemblies. Above the assemblies and magistrates were two people, **consuls,** regarded as the most powerful people in Rome. The power of the consuls was called the **imperium.** The two consuls ruled for one year before handing over power to newly elected consuls. During their one-year tenure, they were responsible for proposing laws and commanding the armies. The two consuls had to agree on everything. In cases where one consul did not agree with what his partner was doing, he could challenge it. This power to disapprove of decisions is called **vetoing** power.

After a consul completed a term, he could become appointed as a pro-consul. A pro-consul could rule one of the Roman Republic's many territories. This appointment as a pro-consul could make him quite wealthy.

The Fall of the Roman Republic

The Roman Republic continued to grow until it became the major world power. As the Republic grew, so did the problems that came with its expansion. One of the most important conflict was the **Social War** which took place from around 90 BC to 88 BCE.

While the Roman Republic was expanding, it made friends with other cities. These cities became **allies**. And because the Roman Republic had so much power and influence, it demanded tributes from allies. During the times of war, allies fought on the Roman side, as well. After some time, these allies became tired of being allies and demanded to be made citizens of Rome. When their initial demands were rejected, the allies rebelled.

While this was going on, the Roman Senate warned the Roman citizens that it would be dangerous for them to give these allies citizenship, but the Romans didn't listen. Finally, Rome finally granted citizenship to all people in the entire Italian peninsula (except slaves; slaves were not considered to be humans. They were regarded as property).

While all this was happening, a Roman senator named Lucius Sergius Catiline conspired to overthrow the Roman government. A man named Marcus Tullius Cicero found out about his plan and exposed him. Cicero also thought the morals of the Romans had decayed which was affecting the Roman Republic.

Marcus Tullius Cicero

Due to all these problems, in the year 60 BC, three men famous for their bravery in battle named Julius Caesar, Marcus Licinius Crassus, and Gnaeus Pompey came together and formed the **First Triumvirate** also known as the **Gang of Three**. For almost ten years, they controlled both the consulship as well as the military.

Julius Caesar

After Julius Caesar finished his term as consul in 59 BCE, he and his army moved northward into Gaul and Germania. Pompey became the governor of Spain (although he ruled from Rome) while Crassus went to the East to seek fame.

Pompey the Great

After this, Gnaeus Pompey and Julius Caesar started to have disagreements and keep grudges. Pompey was jealous of Julius Caesar. Soon, they went to war. In 48 BC, Julius Caesar defeated Gnaeus Pompey at the battle of Pharsalus. Gnaeus Pompey fled to Egypt but Ptolemy XII, the King of Egypt at the time, found him. Ptolemy killed Gnaeus Pompey once he received news of his arrival. Julius Caesar then returned to Rome and declared himself dictator for life, making him the most powerful man in the Roman Republic.

Death of Pompey

Julius Caesar continued to grow in strength and authority. After some time, many of his enemies started to suspect his authority. They feared that he was going to declare himself king and return Rome to monarchy, so they plotted to assassinate him. So, on the 15th of March in the year 44 BC, Julius Caesar was assassinated. Gaius Cassius and Marcus Brutus led the assassination. March 15th suddenly became one of the most important dates in Roman history after Julius Caesar died.

Julius Caesar's death

After the assassination of Julius Caesar, the Roman Republic crumbled. Mark Antony, Julius Caesar's lieutenant, condemned the assassination and was declared a public enemy.

Mark Antony

The Romans appointed Octavian, the son of Julius Caesar, to challenge Mark Antony in battle. Mark Antony lost the Battle of Mutina, but Octavian later later pardoned him. In the same year, the assassins Brutus and Cassius died. In 43 BC, Octavian, Marcus

Lepidus, and Mark Antony formed the Second Triumvirate and defeated the conspirators.

Marcus Lepidus

One year later, the members of the Second Triumvirate started to have conflicts and went to war against one another. In 31 BC, Octavian defeated Mark Antony and proclaimed himself the **Imperium** of the city of Rome. He also named himself Augustus which loosely means 'above all.' He introduced several reforms to the constitution until in the year 27 BC, and he gave himself the title **Imperator Caesar**, thus establishing himself as the first Emperor of Rome.

Augustus Caesar

The Roman Republic began with the revolution which overthrew the monarchy in the year 509 BC. The Roman Republic lasted for 482 years and ended in the year 27 BC. The Roman Republic replaced the monarchy, while the Roman Empire replaced the Roman Republic.

Chapter 3:
The Roman Empire

Have you heard the saying, "Rome was not built in a day?" Well it's literally true. First Rome started off as a kingdom, then it became a republic, and then it became an empire. After Caesar Augustus denounced the Republic and named himself as the Emperor, Rome kept growing and growing. It expanded so much, and as it kept expanding, the Romans continued to become increasingly ambitious. The Romans wanted to conquer the entire ancient world and expand even beyond the Mediterranean; they wanted to subdue everyone else and establish themselves as the only important city in the empire. When they did, they turned the rest of the empire into provinces and colonies, whose purpose was to provide the city of Rome with whatever Rome wanted. Therefore, Rome became the capital of the Roman Empire. Hundreds of years later, a man called Alexander the Great conquered the same people. However, historians still regard the Roman Empire as the most influential civilization in the history of the world. The Romans were impressive organizers and managers. The Roman Empire lasted 500 years, while the reign of the man who defeated them—Alexander the Great—only lasted 13 years. The Romans did not only care about conquering cities, they also cared about keeping their control, and they did this for a very long time.

As the Roman Empire kept expanding, the empire became too big to be ruled from one place (Rome). Soon after Diocletian became Emperor, he divided the Roman Empire into two empires in the year 285CE: Western Empire and Eastern Empire. When the Western Empire (the one ruled from Rome) later fell, the empire did not completely end. The empire continued in the east as the Byzantine Empire. The Byzantine Empire lasted until 1453 when the Ottoman Empire conquered it. But before all this, let's talk about how the Roman Empire rose to such great heights.

After Caesar Augustus took power, he ruled until his death in 31 BC. During his time as a ruler, he made so many reforms and built so many things that he is one of the most important rulers in history. He secured Rome's borders and greatly expanded the empire. Among his greatest achievements was the commissioning of the Pantheon and establishment of the **Pax Romana**, that is, the Roman Peace (also known as the Pax Augusta). This Roman Peace made sure that the Roman Empire experienced its most peaceful period that lasted 200 years.

Pantheon

After Emperor Augustus died, power passed to Tiberius, his heir. Tiberius was very peaceful, even though he did not command as much authority as his father. After Tiberius died, five more emperors followed in the Julio-Claudian **Dynasty**. A dynasty is a series of rulers from the same family.

After Tiberius came the emperors Caligula, Claudius, and Nero. Emperor Claudius' reign was peaceful, and he continued to expand the Roman Empire in power and in territory, but his own wife eventually killed him.

Claudius

Emperor Caligula started his reign well but turned out to be a wicked emperor in the end. Some historians even say he became insane. His own bodyguards, the

Praetorian Guard, killed him. Emperor Nero was the last of the Julio-Claudian Dynasty. He had a bad reign as well and is one of the more corrupt emperors. He committed suicide in the year 68 CE.

Nero

After Emperor Nero's death, Rome became unstable. There were many conflicts. The next year became one of the most turbulent times in Roman history. It was called The Year of the Four Emperors, because four emperors rose and fell in the space of that one year. The four emperors were Emperor Galba, Emperor Otho, Emperor Vitellius, and Emperor Vespasian. After Emperor Nero died, Galba claimed the throne. He ruled for a very short time because the Romans quickly decided he was unfit to rule. Emperor Galba was cruel and irresponsible. His Praetorian guard murdered him. On the same day that Galba died, Otho ascended the throne. Otho was a good ruler in his very short reign, but one of his generals, Vitellius, betrayed him. General Vitellius envied Emperor Otho and lusted after the throne, so he organized a civil war. Shortly after the war started, Emperor Otho committed suicide. When Otho died, Vitellius was finally able to claim power.

Emperor Vitellius

Considering the way that Emperor Vitellius took power, it only made sense that he was a horrible ruler. He squandered the government's money on parties and other extravagant entertainment. He didn't care about his duties as a ruler. Soon, the people got tired of him and demanded he vacate the throne. When he refused, the legions declared a man named Vespasian as the emperor that they wanted. General Vespasian led an army to Rome and took over the city. His men killed Vitellius, and Vespasian became the emperor. Emperor Vitellius died exactly one year after he became emperor.

Vespasian

For the next hundred years, Rome became more powerful. It became far richer and far stronger than any other city in the world. The Romans conquered cities and expanded their empire. Emperor Vespasian founded the Flavian Dynasty that ruled during these prosperous times. Emperor Vespasian built many monumental buildings and supervised the flourish of the Roman Empire. He started building the famous Colosseum of Rome shortly before he died. After he died, his son took over and completed the building.

Roman Colosseum

While Rome prospered, it also suffered some losses. In the year 79 CE, Mount Vesuvius, a volcanic mountain erupted and destroyed two cities: Pompeii and

Herculaneum. A year later, there was a great fire in Rome. Emperor Titus was a wonderful ruler, and he was able to restore the Roman Empire to greatness even after these setbacks. He died the next year (in 81 CE) after a brief sickness and his brother, Domitian, succeeded him. Domitian also improved Rome's economy and continued the building projects his brother, Titus, started. He fully repaired the parts of the city affected by the great fire, and increased the boundaries of the Roman Empire. Despite all his achievements, the Roman Senate felt that he was too rigid for their liking. They soon turned against him and assassinated him in the year 96 CE.

Domitian

After Domitian, the next five emperors were remarkable rulers; they are known as The Five Good Emperors. They were Nerva who ruled from 98 to 117 CE, Trajan who ruled from 117 to 138 CE, Hadrian who ruled from 138 to 161 CE, Antoninus Pius who ruled from 138 CE to 161 CE, and Marcus Aurelius 161 to 180 CE. During the reigns of the Five Good Emperors, the Roman Empire expanded very much. The Roman army grew very powerful and their territories expanded very far.

Marcus Aurelius

After the rule of the Five Good Emperors which ended with Marcus Aurelius' death, his son, Commodus, inherited the throne and proved to be the most disgraceful emperor Rome ever saw. He squandered Rome's money and neglected his duties as a ruler. His wrestling partners murdered him while having his bath in the year 192 CE. After he died, a man named

Pertinax became the emperor. Some people believe Pertinax killed Commodus. Pertinax then founded the Severan Dynasty which included a succession of kings that ruled until 284 CE.

Commodus

The Crisis of the Third Century

The Pertinax Dynasty ended in the year 235 after Emperor Alexander Severus, the last emperor in the dynasty, was murdered. The Crisis of the Third Century is also known as the **Imperial Crisis**, and it lasted for 49 years. During this time, the Roman Empire was thrown into chaos and confusion, and it eventually divided into three separate empires. These three empires were the Gallic Empire, the Roman Empire, and the Palmyrene Empire. During the 49 years of the Crisis of the Third Century, over 20 emperors rose to power and fell.

Alexander Severus

Emperor Alexander Serverus was a good emperor who made positive impact on the Roman Empire, but the army lost respect for him when they realized that his mother, whom they hated, controlled him. So, when some German tribes planned to attack Rome, Emperor Alexander decided to listen to his mother's advice to pay them for peace instead of going to war. The Roman army had already lost faith in the emperor and felt it was an insult because the Roman army was the strongest in the world. The commanders called Emperor Alexander a coward and assassinated him and his mother. After the emperor died, one of the soldiers named Maximinus Thrax ascended to the throne and became the first of the 20 emperors who would rule Rome for the next 49 years during the Crisis of the Third Century.

The Barracks Emperors

Before the army commanders murdered Emperor Alexander Severus, emperors had always inherited power from their fathers. But this changed after Emperor Alexander and his mother died, and Emperor Maximinus Thrax gained control of the throne.

From then on, emperors became chosen by the army instead of by birth. After an emperor died, his children did not automatically become emperors. Instead, the army would choose the next emperor. The army voted based on how popular he was, how generous he was towards the army, and whether they thought he would be able to rule Rome effectively. The army was not as patient as civilians; once the army thought an emperor was misbehaving or not doing his duties well, they would kill him and vote another emperor.

After Maximinus Thrax became emperor, he ruled for only three-and-a-half years before the army got tired of his constant warfare, both within the Roman Empire and outside. They also thought he did not do enough to protect them from famine and hunger. It was only a matter of time before even the civilians turned against him, so some soldiers went ahead and killed him. After Maximinus Thrax died, 19 other rulers ruled Rome for short tenures until the line of the Barracks Emperors ended in 284 CE when the army killed the last Barrack Emperor.

During the Crisis of the Third Century, two leaders were tired of the way things were going so they broke away to form their own empires. In the year 260 CE, Postumus, the governor of Upper and Lower Germania, rebelled and created the Gallic Empire. The Gallic Empire consisted of Germania, Gaul, Hispania, and Britannia (now called the United Kingdom). Ten years later, in the year 270 CE, a woman named Queen Zenobia of Palmyra rebelled and broke away to form the Palmyrene Empire which consisted of all the cities from Syria all the way to Egypt.

Queen Zenobia

Throughout the Crisis of the Third Century, the Roman Emperors were too busy fighting and killing one another that they did not notice the Palmyrene Empire and the Gallic Empire had broken away and reduced the size of the Roman Empire. This reduction continued until Emperor Aurelian reunited the empire after defeating the Gallic and Palmyrene breakaway empires and bringing them back under Roman control.

After the army killed the last Barrack Emperor, Emperor Diocletian rose to power. He thought the problems that led to the secession of the Palmyrene and the Gallic Empires were due to the size of the Roman Empire. The Roman Empire had become so big that it was difficult to rule the whole empire from Rome, so he decided to split it into two empires. The two empires were called the Western Roman Empire and the Eastern Roman Empire. The Eastern Roman Empire was also called the Byzantine Empire.

Emperor Diocletian

Emperor Diocletian also tried to solve the problem of succession during his reign. He thought the act of waiting until an emperor died before the Romans chose a new emperor caused problems in leadership, so he decreed a successor must be chosen at the beginning of an Emperor's rule. The Romans then chose General

Maxentius and Emperor Constantine to rule after Emperor Diocletian's reign. Emperor Diocletian did not rule until his death, but he retired voluntarily in the year 305 CE. However, when he died six years later, Emperors Maxentius and Constantine started a civil war.

Constantine the Great

The civil war lasted from 311 CE to 312 CE and ended when Emperor Constantine defeated Emperor Maxentius at the Battle of the Milvan Bridge. After his victory, Emperor Constantine believed Jesus Christ was responsible for his success. He then introduced

Christianity into the Roman Empire. He decided which books were in the collection of religious books we now call the Bible.

Emperor Constantine made the Roman Empire prosperous again. After conquering Emperor Maxentius, he ruled over the Byzantine Empire and the Western Roman Empire. He built the famous city Constantinopole and reformed the Roman Military. Because of his achievements as a great emperor, he later became known as Constantine the Great.

Chapter 4:
How the Romans
Conquered Britain

Before the Romans conquered Britain, a tribe, called the Celtics, ruled the Britons. When the Roman Empire expanded and became very big, Romans turned their eyes towards Britain. They wanted Britain's precious natural resources, and they knew that the Britons were stubborn people. It was not going to be easy for them. The Romans first invaded Britain in the year 55 BC, but it would be another 100 years before the Romans could fully conquer the Britons.

The First Roman Invasion

In the year 55 BC (55 years before Jesus Christ was born), Julius Caesar led two Roman legions (that is, two large units of the Roman army) to Britain and invaded it. Julius Caesar sent a part of his army to lead a first battle so he could follow up later. His plan was to deceive the Britons to engage the first part of the army with full force, so when they became tired, he would lead his reinforcements and finish them off. But when the first

Roman ships neared Britain, they found out there was no place to land.

Julius Caesar invasion of Britain

From the hills, the Britons attacked the Roman soldiers who decided to swim ashore. The Romans had to wade to land with their heavy weapons and armor which slowed them down. When some of them finally made it to the coast of Britain, they engaged the Britons in a fierce, bloody battle in the shallow water. The waves of the beach affected the Romans, as they were not used to such conditions.

After a long brutal fight, the Britons managed to assemble themselves into a formation that forced the

Romans to flee. Julius Caesar then attacked the Britons. On some days, the Britons were winning, and other days the Romans had the advantage, yet after several days of fighting, Julius Caesar saw that he could not win against the Britons who were more familiar with their rainy weather. He decided that he had had enough deaths, so he gathered what was left of his army and sailed back to the Roman Empire in Gaul.

The Second Roman Invasion

After failing in the first invasion, Julius Caesar decided to wait one year to prepare and plan a stronger attack. This time he took a bigger army of five well-trained legions and sailed to Britain. The legions consisted of about 30,000 infantry soldiers (on foot) and 2,000 cavalrymen (horse riders).

Julius Caesar sailed across the River Thames and launched an attack on the Britons. His failure was even worse than the first time. The harsh weather and strong winds affected his troops and gave the Britons the advantage. After another brutal fight and no winner, the British decided to pay tribute to Rome. Once this happened, the Romans decided to leave in peace. This peace lasted for almost 100 years.

The Third Roman Invasion

A hundred years after the peace treaty, Emperor Claudius organized the third Roman Invasion of Britain in 43 BCE with over 20 legions in the army. General Aulus Plautius led the largest groups of legions. He led four legions with 25,000 men and 25,000 auxiliary soldiers. They crossed the Boulogne Channel in three divisions, landing at Richborough, Dover, and Lympne. They fought the biggest battle on the banks of the River Medway, close to Rochester. It went on for two days before the Celtic tribes retreated. Eleven British kings immediately surrendered to the Roman army, while King Caratacus engaged the 20th legion in a short battle. The legion easily defeated King Caratacus, and he fled to Wales.

While in Wales, King Caratacus planned resistance from the Roman armies, and even though the Romans easily claimed several territories in Britain, some tribes resisted. King Caratacus went to battle again with the Romans at River Severn in BCE 51. He lost the battle and again escaped. Caractacus ran away and hid in the camp of a tribe called Brigantes but the Brigantes queen soon betrayed and exposed him. The Romans then captured Caratacus and sent him back to Rome as a slave.

Nine years later, in 51 BCE, a king of the Iceni tribe, King Prasutagus, who had signed a treaty with the

Romans before, died. His wife, Queen Boudicca, wanted to remain at peace with the Romans, but when the Romans told her to hand over her late husband's lands to them, she refused. This decision angered the Romans, and they attacked her people. During the attack, they plundered the Iceni land and took Queen Boudicca's two daughters.

Queen Boudicca

After the attack, Queen Boudicca avenged her loss. She sought the help of another tribe, the Trinovantes, and they joined forces together. By this time, London was already part of the Roman Empire, so the joint forces of Queen Boudicca and the Trinovantes attacked London and set it on fire. They also attacked Colchester and St. Albans.

When the Romans saw what the forces did to their provinces, they knew they had to take action, so they gathered the largest army in the history of the Roman Empire. They killed anybody who they thought was their enemy. They attacked Queen Boudicca with extreme force. Queen Boudicca had more soldiers than the Romans (she had 200,000 warriors), but the Romans were better trained and had better weapons and armor than her soldiers. So, when both sides clashed in a fierce battle, the Romans won. When Queen Boudicca saw she would lose the war, she poisoned herself so the Romans would not capture her and send her into slavery.

After Queen Boudicca's defeat, the Romans rebuilt London and made it an important city. Before Queen Boudicca burned Colchester, the city had been the British Province seat of governance in the Roman Empire, but after the revolt, London became the seat of governance.

Chapter 5:
Ancient Roman Culture

The Roman civilization lasted for about 1200 years, the longest in history. The Romans conquered many cities, and with each conquest, they learned from the people they conquered and used the knowledge to develop their empire. The Roman culture was a combination of many cultures.

Classes of People in Ancient Rome

In ancient Rome, especially during the monarchy and the Republican era, four classes of people lived in Rome. These classes were the aristocrats who were the highest class in Rome; the equestrians who were the knights (it was an honor to be a knight in the old days); the common citizens, and the slaves were the lowest class of people and regarded as property.

The equestrians, or "equites," were either born into rich families or were people who became rich. They included traders, government builders, and bankers. The common citizens included farmers, industrial workers, and every other person in the city that was not rich. Slaves did not have any free will, and had to work harder than everybody else for little or no pay. Their owners usually released them from bondage when they became old. Some slaves were gladiators. Gladiators were trained to become fighters to entertain the people. They typically fought to the death. Other slaves worked in rich homes as doorkeepers, litter-bearers (carried people around in "vehicles" like palanquins), messengers, and servants. Some slaves who were of Greek origin were teachers.

Slaves carrying their master

Religion

Most Romans had similar religious beliefs, irrespective of which social class they belonged to. They believed that the gods were involved in their everyday lives, and so they were very serious about their religious beliefs. They organized festivals, fancy parties, and other celebrations to honor the gods. The Romans believed that if they made the gods happy, then their gods would be happy with them as well, and would make them happy by blessing them.

At the time of the birth of Jesus, and after he died, the Roman Empire ruled the entire Mediterranean. Followers of Christ worshiped only the Christian God and did not join in the festivals to other gods, so the Romans considered them unpatriotic. The result of this distrust is that many Christians were persecuted, crucified, or sometimes caught and killed by animals to entertain the Romans.

Despite all this, Christianity continued across the Roman Empire. A great change took place when Constantine I became emperor. He moved the capital of the empire to Byzantium, converted to Christianity, and protected Christians from harm. Later in the empire, many people stopped believing in the ancient gods and became Christians, but the majority of the Roman Empire still worshipped and honored their gods.

Food

Poor people ate plant-based meals rather than meat. The Romans did not have breakfast. Rich people ate dinner before four in the afternoon and had meals from three to ten hours before then. Whenever visitors came to dinner, slaves brought the visitors to make sure they were on time. They loved to eat grapes for dessert. They also ate clams and oysters.

Engineering and Architecture

The Romans built wonderful roads and bridges. They built about 50,000 miles (about 80,000 km) of hard-surfaced highways, mostly because they needed their military men to be able to move about with ease. Each time they conquered a new city, they built a road from that city back to Rome (which is where the saying, "all roads lead to Rome" came from). They built their roads in lines as straight as possible, and their roads had gutters. Along the side of the road, the Romans built road signs called milestones. Milestones did not give any information about other towns in the area, but they told how far from Rome they were. The

Romans built their roads so well that even after the Roman Empire fell, the roads continued to be useful in Europe.

Ancient road in Rome named The Appian Way

They used mosaics to decorate the floors of their buildings and painted their walls.

One of the most iconic buildings in the world is the Roman Pantheon, which was once a temple for all the Roman gods. The Pantheon is a domed brick-faced concrete rotunda standing at 43.3 meters high and 43.3 meters wide with a rectangular portico, a type of roof, and has granite columns. Another great structure which is still standing today is the Colosseum. The Colosseum was once an amphitheater where people gathered to watch gladiators fight.

Arts, Language, and Music

The Romans spoke Latin, a language that was based on the Etruscan alphabet. The Latin alphabet is the basis for the major world languages today: Portuguese, French, Italian, and even English.

Face of the Emperor Constantine and Latin script

The Romans wrote plays and kept the Phoenician alphabet they developed from the Phonenician civilization. Roman music was an important part of their lives, influenced by Etruscan and Greek music. Songs were an integral part of every social event, and Roman music accompanied spectacles and events in the arena.

Conclusion

The Fall of the Roman Empire

Rome ruled a greater part of Europe and the Mediterranean for over a thousand years. However, the Roman Empire began to decline starting around 200 BCE. Two centuries (two hundred years) later, at around 400 BCE, the Roman Empire had grown so big that it struggled with its size. Even though Emperor Diocletian had divided it into two, Constantine the Great had reunited them back, so the empire continued to grow.

Rome reached its highest power in 117 BCE when Emperor Trajan was in power. By that time, the entire coastline along the Mediterranean Sea was part of the Roman Empire, including Spain, Italy, France, southern Britain, Turkey, Israel, Egypt, and northern Africa. The Roman Empire stretched and stretched until it began to crack on the inside. The city of Rome finally fell in 476 BCE.

Many thought the city of Rome was unconquerable. However, in 410 BCE, a Germanic barbarian tribe called the Visigoths invaded the city. They looted the treasures, killed and enslaved many Romans, and destroyed many buildings. For the first time in 800 years, the city of Rome had been sacked.

In 476 BCE, a Germanic barbarian named Odoacer became the king of Italy. He then attacked Rome, won the battle, then forced the last emperor of Rome, Emperor Romulus Augustulus, to vacate his position and give up his crown. Emperor Romulus Augustulus' surrender marked the end of the Western Roman Empire and plunged Europe into what is known as the Dark Ages.

Roman emperor, Romulus Augustulus, gives his crown to Odoacer

With the fall of Rome, Europe changed. Rome was civilized and had provided a strong government, education, and culture. Now that Rome had fallen, barbarianism took over Europe. The Eastern Roman

Empire, however, continued on as the Byzantine Empire for another 1000 years until 1453 CE, when the Ottoman Empire defeated Constantinople, which was its capital.

Roman Legacy

Nothing lasts forever. But even though Rome fell, its legacy lives on. The inventions and innovations that the Roman Empire started continue to be useful in the world today. Roman culture directly affected the Western culture. The construction of roads and buildings, indoor plumbing, and fast-drying cement were either invented or improved upon by the Romans. Even the calendar that we use today is merely an improvement and modification of the one that Julius Caesar created back in the day; the names of the days of the week (in the Roman languages) and months of the year also come from Ancient Rome.

The Romans were always open to learning, and so they made sure they borrowed from, and improved upon, everything they found useful among the regions they conquered. You are not wrong if you call them the perfect copycats. The Roman Empire left an enduring legacy which continues to reflect in the lives of people in today's world.

More from us

Visit our book store at: www.dinobibi.com

History series

Travel series

Made in the USA
Las Vegas, NV
14 March 2022